To _____

From _____

Garfield's

TOP TEN

tom CAT foolery

Created by Jim Davis
Written by Jim Kraft and Mark Acey
Illustrated by Paws, Inc.

Andrews and McMeel
A Universal Press Syndicate Company
Kansas City

ISBN: 0-8362-0931-1

Garfield's

TOP
TEN

tom CAT ∧ foolery

BY JIM DAVIS

TOP TEN REASONS
TO GO OFF YOUR DIET

10. Rice cakes cause mange

9. Cheesecake population needs to be thinned

8. Do-it-yourself liposuction available in near future

7. Ignored desserts will develop low self-esteem

6. Half-off coupon for fat farm has expired

5. Shamu was a nobody before he put on weight

4. Less mutant leftovers spawning in your refrigerator

3. Love handles provide great place for setting snacks

2. Sumo wrestlers earn big bucks

1. A tummy is a terrible thing to waste!

TOP TEN SIGNS THAT YOUR CAT IS A "GARFIELD"

10. Your pet food bill surpasses the national debt

9. He gets a court order requiring you to pamper him

8. Dogs in your neighborhood get anonymous hate mail

7. Mice hold conventions at your place

6. Your plants die mysterious deaths

5. Veterinarians pay you not to visit them

4. He puts a combination lock on your refrigerator

3. He's sometimes mistaken for Rhode Island

2. He tries to have **you** fixed

1. Can't tell if he's sleeping or dead

GARFIELD'S TOP TEN FAVORITE COUNTRY PET TUNES

10. Daddy Sang Bass, Mama Had Worms

9. Lipstick On Your Flea Collar, Cheatin' On Your Mind

8. I Burp As Much In Texas As I Did In Tennessee

7. Call Me A Hairball Tomorrow, But Feed Me Tonight

6. Bubba Shot The Litterbox

5. Odie From Muskogee

4. Mamas, Don't Let Your Kittens Grow Up To Be Professional Wrestlers

3. Walk Softly On This Tail Of Mine

2. You Used To Be My Chew Toy, But I Used To Have Some Teeth

1. Honky-Tonk Tabby (Gettin' Old...Feelin' Flabby)

TOP TEN GREATEST INVENTIONS EVER ACCORDING TO GARFIELD

10. remote control

9. dog muzzle

8. donuts

7. coffeemaker

6. comics

5. sleep sofa

4. back scratcher

3. microwave

2. pizza

1. microwave pizza

TOP TEN EXCUSES
FOR BREAKING A DATE

10. "Don't know how I forgot this engagement at Buckingham Palace."

9. "My cousin really needs my kidney."

8. "I'd let you talk to the space aliens, but for some reason they can only communicate with me."

7. "It's a hair thing. I know you'll understand."

6. "That must have been one of my other personalities."

5. "Everything before the accident is a blank."

4. "I just remembered—I'm married."

3. "I know it's last-minute, but I've decided to change my sex."

2. "Sorry, I had you confused with someone attractive."

1. "I'm probably not contagious, but..."

GARFIELD'S TOP TEN ROMANTIC NICKNAMES FOR HIMSELF

10. "Love Chunky"

9. "Sweet Jowls"

8. "The Round Mound of Romance"

7. "Garfield von Studly"

6. "Sizzle Whiskers"

5. "Orange Thunder"

4. "Passion Paws"

3. "The Thrillmeister"

2. "Catsanova"

1. "Available"

TOP TEN REASONS GARFIELD WILL (PROBABLY) NEVER PLAY IN THE NBA

10. Hates being cooped up in pet carrier during road trips

9. Tough to rebound with guys standing on your tail

8. Goes to sleep on defense...literally

7. Shoots too many hairballs

6. Astronomical wage demands push teams over salary cap

5. Major girth precludes serious hangtime

4. One whiff of locker room, he loses his lunch

3. Notorious trash talker...can't back it up

2. His only moves are toward concession stand

1. For Pete's sake, he's a cat!

TOP TEN REASONS GARFIELD WILL (PROBABLY) NEVER WIN A NOBEL PRIZE

10. Swedish king a nut about cat hairs on the furniture

9. Meant to do life-saving DNA research, but overslept

8. Mooned Bjorn Borg during 1978 Wimbledon final

7. Always bets against the Minnesota Vikings

6. Literary output mostly fan letters to himself

5. Once called Swedes "a bunch of reindeer-rubbing fjord monkeys"

4. Kissinger mouthed-off; gave short, fat winners a bad rep

3. Academy under thumb of Marmaduke lobby

2. Won't come across with the kronor, if you know what I mean

1. Starts to propose peace plan, winds up kicking Odie's butt

TOP TEN SIGNS
THAT YOU'RE REALLY OLD

10. You can play connect-the-dots on your liver spots

9. Went to antique auction...three people bid on you

8. Used to put cream in your coffee; now put formaldehyde

7. You knew Alexander the Great when he was just mediocre

6. Still growing hair, but only in your nose

5. You sprinkle tenderizer on your applesauce

4. They ask to check your bags, and you're not carrying any

3. Prostate now the size of a pumpkin

2. Your birth certificate is written in hieroglyphics

1. You've even got wrinkles on your teeth!

TOP TEN SIGNS
THAT YOU'RE REALLY FAT

10. You have this tremendous urge to graze

9. Waiters bring you the dessert menu first

8. Your new house is a blimp hangar

7. You sweat butter

6. When you turn over, it registers on the Richter scale

5. A NASA satellite starts orbiting you

4. Someone tries to climb your north slope

3. You wonder if you still have feet

2. Even your mom starts calling you "Moby"

1. You think Garfield is in pretty good shape!

TOP TEN TOYS
FOR DELINQUENT CATS

10. "Buffy, The Inflatable Love Kitten"

9. Studded-leather scratching post

8. Officer McGruff punching bag

7. Tiny brass knuckles

6. Yarn noose

5. Stiletto with can opener attachment

4. "Bag o' Frightened Middle-Class Mice"

3. Ball of piano wire

2. Birdzooka

1. Puppy on a string

TOP TEN REASONS DOGS ARE EXPELLED FROM OBEDIENCE SCHOOL

10. Drinking from faculty toilet

9. Never turning in homework. Always claiming owner ate it

8. Licking themselves during the Pledge of Allegiance

7. Violating school dress code with "Cats Suck" T-shirt

6. Carjacking

5. Playing hooky when they should be playing dead

4. Cutting line at the hydrant

3. Continuous barking during study hall

2. Hiding crib notes on back of flea collar

1. Ripping out throat of trainer

JON ARBUCKLE'S
TOP TEN PICK-UP LINES

10. "Excuse me, have you seen my Nobel Prize around here anywhere?"

9. "I'm still into macramé. How about you?"

8. "You look like a woman with low standards."

7. "You've certainly got the figure for that dumpy cashier's outfit."

WILL WORK FOR DATE

6. "When I saw you, I lost control of all my bodily functions."

5. "Ever been hit on by a cartoon character?"

4. "Are you as lonely and depressed as I am?"

3. "I have very few communicable diseases."

2. "Please. I'm begging you."

1. "Uh...uh...um...duh...cough..."

GARFIELD'S TOP TEN COMPLAINTS ABOUT HIS STRIP

10. Buried in back while sissy disasters hog front page

9. Has typecast him as a cat

8. Can't get rid of that newsprint smell

7. Low budget means sharing dressing room with Doc Boy

6. Bum knees from doing so many stunts

5. Jon often blows lines; panels must be re-drawn

4. Word balloon once fell and nearly killed him

3. Drawing makes him look ten pounds heavier

2. Hates having to be "on" every day

1. Too much Odie, not enough babes

TOP TEN THINGS GARFIELD IS MOST OFTEN MISTAKEN FOR

10. Pumpkin with feet

9. Rare striped hippo

8. Reincarnation of Orson Welles

7. The Blob's fuzzy cousin

6. Fur-capped mountain

I RESEMBLE THAT REMARK

5. Guy with high-pitched voice who used to sing with Paul Simon

4. Tiger who has let himself go

3. The Orange Bowl

2. Heathcliff

1. Someone who gives a whoopty-doo

GARFIELD'S TOP TEN EXCUSES FOR NOT CATCHING A MOUSE

10. "I thought it was just a squeaky dustball."

9. "I tore a rotator cuff."

8. "The mouse had a restraining order."

7. "I left my instincts in another life."

6. "Gandhi made me not do it."

5. "I come from a lazy home."

4. "He maced me."

3. "You mean mice **aren't** an endangered species?"

2. "I'm on a no-vermin diet."

1. "Would **you** stick a live rodent in **your** mouth?"

TOP TEN WAYS
GARFIELD LIKES HIS COFFEE

10. Hot

9. Hair-free

8. Non-crunchy

7. One barrel at a time

6. Doughnut-ready

5. So caffeinated it jumps out of the cup and slaps him

4. Sucked straight out of the filter

3. Intravenously

2. Strong enough to sit up and bark

1. With a 12-course breakfast

TOP TEN REASONS TO OWN A CAT INSTEAD OF A DOG

10. No need to drool-proof your home

9. Cat has absolutely no romantic interest in your leg

8. Nothing spooks a burglar like stepping on a cat

7. Dog breath actually killed a guy in Utah

6. Cat always returns your car with a full tank

5. Cat will keep yard free of pesky songbirds

4. Cat won't drag you out into blizzard just to piddle on a tree

3. Ever seen **Cujo**?

2. Dogs...Fetch, roll over, sit up and beg; Cats...Drive, balance checkbook, give CPR

1. Garfield. Odie. Case closed

TOP TEN WAYS GARFIELD IS HELPING THE U.S. SPACE PROGRAM

10. Attends all NASA bake sales

9. Gathers important scientific data from "Star Trek" reruns

8. Regularly volunteers Odie for mission to Uranus

7. Is a judge at NASA cheerleader tryouts

6. Entertains astronauts with killer impression of Werner von Braun

5. Teaches NASA class on how to pick up space babes

4. Every Garfield comic strip contains subliminal message "Throw more money at Mars!"

3. Allows UFOs to crash at his place on weekends

2. Watches all space launches on TV to make sure rocket is not upside-down

1. Free Garfield air freshener in every shuttle!

TOP TEN THINGS GARFIELD WOULD DO IF HE HEADED THE CIA

10. Have lab develop fruit-flavored cyanide capsules

9. Get Michael Jackson to write snappy CIA song

8. Take Odie for a drive; surprise him with the old "ejector seat"

7. Put on disguise, go through cafeteria line twice!

6. Hold debriefings at Ben and Jerry's

5. Prevent Iraq from developing "Clapper" capability

4. Plant mole inside Kentucky Fried Chicken to learn secret recipe

3. Impress the babes with all the classified stuff he knows

2. Bug the suction-cup Garfield in Castro's car

1. Tap Mickey's phone

GARFIELD'S TOP TEN EUPHEMISMS FOR "FAT"

10. "corporally well-endowed"

9. "sofa-bodied"

8. "Santa-waisted"

7. "seam-testing"

6. "Ebertine"

5. "up-sized petite"

4. "sun-blotting"

3. "experiencing a cell surplus"

2. "dinner-friendly"

1. "Orson-esque"

TOP TEN FINE DINING FAUX PAS

10. Gargling your aperitif

9. Bribing the maitre d' with a roll of nickels

8. Asking the waiter for a spittoon

7. Showing your culinary savoir faire by ordering chocolate mousse sans antlers

6. Clipping your toenails at the table

5. Pulling up to the valet parking area in a tractor

4. Telling the chef his chicken was "almost as good as the Colonel's"

3. Plunking your false teeth into your finger bowl

2. Displaying what a coffee connoisseur you are by ordering a cup of "Al Pacino"

1. Bringing your own possum in case it's not on the menu

JON ARBUCKLE'S TOP TEN FAVORITE TV TALK SHOW TOPICS

10. Women who love men who love bunny slippers

9. Battered pet owner syndrome

8. Mimes with facial ticks

7. 101 uses for dental floss

6. Elvis impersonators meet Urkel look-alikes

5. Portly babes modeling bikinis

4. "I spent prom night organizing my sock drawer"

3. Men who want to be reincarnated as Huntz Hall

2. Celebrity bedwetters

1. Disco! Disco! Disco!

EXCERPTS FROM GARFIELD'S TOP TEN WEIRDEST FAN LETTERS

10. "I've been watching you and I know where you live. I just don't know where I live. Can you help me?"

9. "My Uncle Clarence has a bedsore that's shaped like you."

8. "Has Odie had tongue augmentation?"

7. "I'm glad that Garfield hates spiders. My ex-husband was a spider. The bum."

6. "I want to have your litter."

5. "I'm not changing my underwear till you get your own prime-time TV show."

4. "Were you really Shirley MacLaine in a previous life?"

3. "Enclosed is my recipe for hairball chowder."

2. "Before you were famous, didn't you appear fur-less in a skin flick?"

1. "Arf! Arf! Arf! Die! Arf! Arf!"

GARFIELD'S TOP TEN
STRESS FACTORS IN LIFE

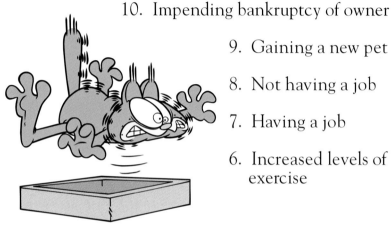

10. Impending bankruptcy of owner

9. Gaining a new pet

8. Not having a job

7. Having a job

6. Increased levels of exercise

5. Disruption of sleep cycle

4. Major injury to teddy bear

3. Incarceration in pet cage

2. Separation from TV set

1. Death of refrigerator

TOP TEN WAYS GARFIELD HAS CHANGED THE WORLD

10. Dogs finding it harder to buy handguns

9. Nuclear superiority now less important than a good nap

8. More cats being elected to public office

7. American flag now red, white, and orange

6. Comics page no longer controlled by Marmaduke cartel

5. Farmers making big bucks raising pasta

4. Diet gags brought down Iron Curtain

3. Scientists working harder to find the cure for exercise

2. Suction cup doll now standard equipment on all new cars

1. Helped build a fatter, lazier America

GARFIELD'S TOP TEN
EPITAPHS FOR HIMSELF

10. "This should only happen to a dog"

9. "I can use the rest"

8. "Back in a minute"

7. "You should look this good"

6. "Hey! Watch your feet!"

5. "I had the time of my lives"

4. "Just your average giant of the entertainment industry"

3. "He ate and slept it all"

2. "Your loss"

1. "Big fat hereafter deal"